THIS MUSIC
POEMS

Karen Holden
Preface by Michael Ventura

LettersAt3amPress

Also by Karen Holden

Book of Changes

THIS MUSIC

POEMS

Karen Holden

This Music
Copyright © 2014 by Karen Holden
Publisher's Preface copyright © 2014 by Michael Ventura

ISBN 978-0-9914648-2-1
Library of Congress Number 2014944269

Published in 2014 by LettersAt3amPress: 6923 Indiana Avenue #266, Lubbock, TX 79413. E-address: editor@3amproductions.org

Publisher/Editors: Jazmin Aminian, Michael Ventura
Editor-at-Large: Rebekah J. Morton

Cover design by Karen Holden

All rights reserved. No part of this book may be reproduced, stored in, or introduced into a retrieval system, or transmitted, in any form or by any means (electronic, mechanical, photocopying, recording or otherwise) without the written permission of the publishers.

Thanks to the following magazines in which several of these poems first appeared:

Michigan Quarterly Review XLIX.4 (Fall 2010): "Desafinado: Antonio Carlos Jobim" and "Pavane Pour Une Infante Défunte: Maurice Ravel"

Black Clock 6 (2006): "Instrumental II" (published as "Instrumental")

Sonora Review 41/42 (Spring 2002): a section from "Sonata No. 14 in C-sharp Minor, *Quasi una Fantasia*, Op. 27, No. 2 (*Moonlight*): Ludwig van Beethoven"

for
John A and Cheryl J

and in memory of
Ling Po

it's to win particular hearts,
to stir an abiding affection for this music,

Robert Duncan

Contents

Publisher's Preface	11
Köln Concert: Keith Jarrett	15
String Quintet in C, Op. 163: Franz Schubert	18
String Quartet in F Major, Op. 96 (*American*): Antonín Dvořák	23
Capriccio in C-sharp Minor, Op. 76: Johannes Brahms	28
Six Suites for Unaccompanied Cello: Johann Sebastian Bach	30
'Round Midnight: Thelonious Monk	36
Pavane Pour Une Infante Défunte: Maurice Ravel	39
In a Sentimental Mood: Duke Ellington	41
Instrumental II: James Taylor	43
Desafinado: Antonio Carlos Jobim	44
Shine: Ford Dabney, Cecil Mack, Lew Brown	45
Requiem, Op. 48: Gabriel Fauré	46
Kol Nidrei, Op. 47, Adagio on Hebrew Melodies: Max Bruch	54
Aegean Sea: Vasilis Dimitriou	64
Fantasia on a Theme by Thomas Tallis: Ralph Vaughan Williams	66
Sonata No. 14 in C-sharp Minor, *Quasi una Fantasia*, Op. 27, No. 2 (*Moonlight*): Ludwig van Beethoven	67
Lullaby: George Gershwin	73
Carly and Carole: Eumir Deodato	75
Two Studies on Ancient Greek Scales: Harry Partch	76
Thanksgiving: George Winston	78
The Four Seasons: Antonio Vivaldi	79
Synchrony No. 2: Moondog (Louis Hardin)	83
Notes on the Music	85
Acknowledgments	91

Publisher's Preface

Karen Holden's poetry creates a space of listening. A space for listening. There is a quiet at the center of each poem that makes you expectant, alert.

What happens in this collection is music—but more than the music of Holden's words or the music of instruments made of wood, brass, and skins. This: Music as behavior, behavior as music…music translated to behavior, behavior translated to music…all with Holden's exquisite tension of syntax, as in the necessary tension of a violin's strings.

I love the immediacy of Karen Holden's poetry and her contemplative range. Tender but tough-minded, the quietude of *This Music* belies her boldness of conception and her adventurous grasp of forms. Every page is unexpected.

Michael Ventura

THIS MUSIC

Köln Concert: Keith Jarrett

I think with my hands.
        Maya Lin

Part I

Your hands, curved on the keyboard
the fine line of light around your face
the folds your shirt makes, like folds
in the robes of a medieval monk
equally illuminated by some inner song
like fields furrowed, or river rapids
folding in on themselves

I want to hide myself in one of those folds
music or material, your sleeve or eyelid
the swift-like curve of hair around your ear
fold myself into something that itself will float
will furrow, will finally be carried, by current, away

Two rivers moving against each other
the sound of original *aleph*, your moans, currents
deep and buoying into a blue unknown by any
but broken hearts

Part IIa

How still the moment is

Only music eddying, your arms
suspended in a star of light so perfect my throat tightens
around the sound, tries to hold it, to hold this longing, the subtle
movement of your eyes closing in response to the caress
of a perfect musical line

Part IIb

The light makes you
paints an eye against your cheek
creates creases that speak your shape as something
made by hands, molded and hewn—that *poeia*
derived of a great possession

The bridge your hands make as they span the keyboard
cuts you in two: sky and earth, river and sky
your arms lift to wings on either side of your head

I want to lift those long hands, place my lips against the inner wrist
run my cheek along your fingers as the music curves against me
my head cupped in your shoulder, your hand cupping my head
captured there, in the kind reflective light as music maneuvers
my physiology so pain cannot come and death cannot come and time
is sliced finger fine, ribbons out from the keyboard pure as light

Part IIc

You play the last note
a note you did not know when you began
something deeper than emotion, below all fields
of feeling with its nostalgic grime
then you stand, step away from the piano, move
into the light. This clarity
carried to bone, to cells, and deeper still
into an unnamable liquid space that floats it all

You stand
walk away from that resonating note
without trying to hold it. This lingering
glittering music turns feeling into landscape
late sunlight, an auburn autumn plain, turns longing
into river, rising and rushing. This music through
your hands—more than the body can contain

String Quintet in C, Op. 163: Franz Schubert

At the Abbaye Saint Michel de Cuxa in Prades, France

I. *Allegro ma non troppo*

Enormous muscular beauty, this rising sound
the heaving flanks of horses newly sweated
their ligaments and tendons, thick braided tails
hands that did the delicate work, same upon
the strings, thick themed and resonant, the gyring
notes entwined as memory in music or dusty
cords of light through end of day rose windows
an altar blanched of color and darkness moving
down the stone to sorrow

slight sorrow, and if water, stream
its sine wave currents weaving through a meadow
tall with grass and gray-barked apple trees, thick
limbs twisting into intricate branch, bending, finally down to fruit

As landscape, hillocks, undulating, and sky
the nearest dawn, the time when one's unclear if blackness
lightens or light withdraws

Purple, all its blue and red, but mostly light
lavender veins etched on eyelid, a newly shadowed
bruise and dusty plums, their dark skins matte and frosted, bright
beneath, deep undertone that quickens strings to sing

As action it is lifting, like air or smoke or ether, like
standing up or raising eyes or shouldering an unknown weight
and hands, palms up to supplicate

If this music were a distance, some stop halfway short of long
it walks a tightrope, cuts what is remembered from what will
never be, neither cold nor hot but fragrant as thyme
warmed by sun and newly watered in the field
not in love with words as sound but meaning, sheer substance
language just before it leaves the mouth

II. *Adagio*

She says: if only
one piece of music may survive, a single
movement, say
let it be this adagio

Let the earth swallow the rest
of sound, the ears die to these slow full
crescendos, long-stringed chords, vibrate down
to the soundless under sound, turn water
inside out

Let the final moments of all there is
of earth, increased by pleasure, diminished
by pain, be dark
undertow of these two cellos, these
violins plucking and plaintive, a single
viola weaving it all

Let it sing the second chance creation
as if to unfind sleep, let it carry on into the east
gallop across the Pyrenees into a nether
world of music at the rim of meaning, let it
drag this world into its voiceless future
let it be as it was in the beginning:
perfect

III. *Scherzo (Presto) and Trio (Andante sostenuto)*

Some world in the making
mutable and without edge, quick cut
an alchemy of stone to silence
silence to sound, sweep of notes some place
east of knowing, each note a step closer
each lifting note a gesture
                dragonflies sketching a summer sky

Ten centuries of heartbeat, and wing
plunk, plunk the cello strings, catch
ancient starlight, horses racing, the rise, the fall
contained right here, within these walls

IV. *Allegretto*

Suspension bridge rocking
between the cellos and the violins—viola
then whistling space before the echo and the call

Bronze tones as notes near completion
then hold on, articulate in twisting harmonies
sheer physical exertion pulls sound from eternity

those braiding currents, thick urgency of pulsing form
a tower rising above the cypress into sky, in memory, as music
soaks the air where spirit flies

String Quartet in F Major, Op. 96 (*American*): Antonín Dvořák

I. *Allegro ma non troppo*

    Brown as soil six feet deep and wider than the world we came from

As grass rustles and nickers, shimmies and snags, the dance it does
    rubbing and clicking, a contrapuntal round
As wind rolls the golden blanket of it, crickets and katydids, the hum
    of gnats and flies colors the fields with sound
As roots grab soil six feet deep, stems shudder, starlings and grackles
    rise into a plate blue sky, quail and pheasants scour the ground

    Brown as the bare feet of boys, the knotty hands of women
    snatching the stalks men swinging the scythes

As sunlight, sunlight douses it all, dust rising, June bugs flying, the
    grain heads as they fall, and in the neighbor's field a mule-drawn
    reaper, boys behind to grab and shock the sheaves
As later at the threshing, most violent of all, the whack of flail the
    shattered heads the rake against the straw
As winnowing, the grain and chaff shunted to baskets thrown against
    the air and what the wind refuses, ours to mill

    Brown as bread baked by hands burned brown by the sun

II. *Lento*

A reel within the field
a waltz in measured time
shoulder to shoulder weaving slow
in rows, a line of dancers
amid the native dance of grass
progressing forward then
down again in rote of dance and harvest
slow swinging scythe and sickle lithe
against the brittle stems

Eyes touch across the tawny heads
shimmering in summer air, a glance
as hot and slow as sun between the shoulder
blades reflecting off the cutting blades
a hat pushed back an apron damp
with sweat and sway then bend and lift
bend and tie, bow and dip make dancing
of this work, the rhythmic call from row to row
from scythe to scythe a staggered *hello*

Winding as we might at harvest dance
serpentine figures in the waving grass, sun
arcing like clock hands across the sky
worn cloth, worn arms, bare feet or broken boots
crows chop the air with cries, worn hands, wind
dies, the evening grows the grasses fall
beneath the blade until the last of all, then hands
upon our knees we bow, we bend exhausted
and bless this bearing earth before we rise

III. *Molto vivace*

Within my music grasses grow
they form a sod a meter deep of memory
from misery and joy, from barley, rye
red winter wheat carried here by countrymen
within their parcels, to grow in ground beneath their feet
Bohemia, in some Midwestern field

They stowed the grain among the folds of linen
wrapped in handkerchiefs, sewn in shirts and carried close
against their breasts, these handfuls bear the beauty of a country
lost, a country rich with food and friends and here I am, again
among my countrymen, hard handed, Slavic toned, standing
on land that feeds another nation, now my own

Far removed from Prague and farther yet New York
those glorious cities I call home, that gave me name and house
my music in halls among those who never plowed a field
in fields that feed my fame my sadness grows like weeds
such cities are rare fruit and it is simple sustenance I need
so I have come to Iowa, I've come to harvest seed

IV. *Vivace ma non troppo*

The wagons came and cut the trails
        the wagons flew across the rutted fields
                the wagons hurtled hard beneath the sky
        they threw up dust, before, behind

Our families thought we'd come this far to die
        but we laid fields in prairie grass that rolled for miles
                the roots twined deep to make a sod
        we cut with blades and turned to face our God

We planted seed we carried near our hearts
        then ringed the fields with trees as we remembered
                more wagons came and cut more trails but we stayed on
        our roots twined deep to make up farm and family

The woodlands planted at the borders of the fields
        left edge for deer and fox, raccoon to rake the night for food
                we always laid a plate for dust-stunned travelers
        stayed on across the years of wheat and famine

The wagons went and then the farms
        the cities cut into the fields, the woodlands paved
                now highways make dark waves
        where we remember planting acres of grain

The wagons come and cut the trails
        the wagons fly across the phantom fields
                the wagons hurtle hard beneath the sky
      they throw exhaust, before, behind

Capriccio in C-sharp Minor, Op. 76: Johannes Brahms

> *There is a place where love begins and a place where love ends—*
> Carl Sandburg

Borrowed room
an old pink quilt, curled
in a corner we waited
out the moon

Planes of your face, first
shadowed then sharp
awash in spreading dawn
intrusion to the night's

Inconstant self, caught in
caprice, a sudden start of mind—
how light the world can be!

The hesitant sun
a wooden floor
this wedge of dust
pink quilt, tucked tight

Your fingers twitching
against the Brahms that
smeared the air, and
where from here?

Is it your hands
or the music I love, better
the music than what death can touch

A ring of was and is and will
be forged in platinum
thin and fine, beginning and end
touching in that brief spell

Your face, your hands
the quilt, the room
and then the sun would
rise and kill the light

Inside my chest while in
your face expression died
we waited out the moon

Six Suites for Unaccompanied Cello: Johann Sebastian Bach

Suite No. 1, G Major

Green leaf, yellow field, blue sky, red clouds. Ghosty grasses backlit with the setting sun etched pale by a saw-edge of sound. A fan of clouds sweeps heavenward, shining, shining, as pine and fir block print the sky. Open field, open tones, notes finger painted from the strings, final splash of vivid poppy and fragile dandelion gone to seed. Day rings her last resonance over this house, music lifts to the cooling sky, drifts higher than the clouds, changes shape on the horizon to sketch the melancholy of sunset, of Sunday, of summer's end, as intricate seed heads shake and bend, impatient before the long and separate night

Suite No. 2, D Minor

Sunset or autumn or yellowing leaves starred from mahogany branch ends of madrone trees. Viburnum and hazelnut, the swipe of color honeysuckle blossoms make—color of sunset, of autumn, the goat leafed, the deep green, the glossy auburn seed, the speechless, the unspeakably sad. Smooth in the palm but cold there, like the last days of autumn air wrapping the trees. A milk-sopped sky heavy as the heart that moves the bow across the strings. Cello mass, the same hard brown as nut and branch—red brown and polished. Mahogany and hazelnut, the heart gone hard and winter near

Suite No. 3, C Major

One man, one cello embraced between his knees—a love affair. Spine and stem of broken leaf, the places where mouth and mind will never meet, large leaps like drumming on open strings, unfretted, arrhythmic heartbeat. His fingers strong against her neck arousing sounds that converge, then part. The warm low pitch that leaps and plunges, ribbons unrestrained through broken chords arising from that womanly form. His hands on her satisfy a single passion, their union exhausted in lonely notes. Expression richens, rises to a dance not meant for dancing, a song not born of voice. He is conjurer, then cad who leaves her each night closed inside her own dark case. Spent instrument of desire, her melody still vibrates

Suite No. 4, E Flat

Sweet respite from the complex day. Simple night unties the knots that mind has made. Unstable, multiple mind whacks again against successive doors that sleep unlatched with her restless fingers, then edges into animated dreams. Her agitation differs from the tensions of awake, is not so black and white. It winds and wanders through the strings, then in and out of time, and if the sound begins to run away, the scene is hard to take, she flips the frame

Suite No. 5, C Minor

To travel a great distance, as hummingbirds do, or winter geese, the sound must rise into a thinning air, must slice the heart of dissonance and resonance, endure no rub, no aggravating buzz of strings, no brooding bow that drags across the music of an anxious mind to slow the flight. The silent lifting wings leave fright behind, dotting the molasses of common life, that street tar softening in summer heat, or quicksand, golden syrup thick on steaming meal. Each note inscribed will tune the eye, will ring austere and scroll through space an ever-forward moving design. Subdued in somber meditation, music that splits illusion with its beak to rend a tiny hole in the texture of melody and harmony, her final descent a sigh

Suite No. 6, D Major

Prelude and gigue, the allemande, courante, gavotte and sarabande.
A weaving dance of voice and wings against an Appalachian spring,
bright green and grassy. A boy's voice changing, cracking from light
to deep, a woman's evening call echoing from peak to peak in broken
harmony while birds cut paper figures within the air's polyphony.
One voice winds out, reels back, the other calling low, then high. Her
hands, the fingers intertwined, the blue grass of these mountains a
remembered lullaby. And cluttering the air in undertone are songbirds
in a frenzied flight, breaking twigs and stealing string and flying from
ground to tree, intention, concentration and bickering, two voices
all business in the gathering. Four voices fly apart, together, lace the
sky with cries and wings until the boy is home, the nest is built, the
movement stilled, the dance complete

'Round Midnight: Thelonious Monk

> **night** *(nīt), n. [AS. niht, neaht, night; compare Ice. nott,*
> *Sw. natt, Dan. nat, Goth. nahts, D. and G. nacht,*
> *Lith. naktis, L. nox, noctis, Gr. nyx, nyktos,*
> *Sans. nakti, nakta, night.]*
>
> Webster's Unabridged Dictionary

I.

In all languages
the same mathematics of sound
beginning with a wail restrained
behind the teeth:
         n a h
                and moving to I
center of the universe, infant's howl
set in motion as music
dark cavern of throat
where voice bounces before becoming word
              clipping chords
rising through the chest as despair rises
bosky and thick, dissonance, assonance
the minor second words and music make
where they meet
           plunk plunked from the piano
             inky and deep:
                  n i g h t

II.

Start and finish meet at middle C
day goes east and night, west
midnight cuts the keyboard, your finger
poised at that round note
                        dark body
a fulcrum
        an onyx stone
halves the dark fruit of knowing, cleaves diminishing from return
transcribes the light

The indigo heart of each flower
bottom drawer of every heart
                        eggplant sheen
slowest moment
        farthest reach, a wound
                that will not heal

Licorice twist of desire
noose that hangs the sun, knotted
                        'round the day
grief that falls away in solitude, and pain, the egg of the moon
turning toward full

III.

Dark notes, growing
dark seed, cracking to root
dark mass blooming in your brain
splitting your hands on the piano
weighing your body to the bed

Voice chaffed, so you turned inward
made music stacked with silence, stuttering
spaces, a clear black sky poked full of holes
by stars in their dying, eighty-eight
keys and each of them Eden

Luminous music growing
beneath odd hats, dark tones
cracking from your fingers, dark
desire blooming in your heart, lightened
by some midnight sun that never sets

After twilight before the dawn
darkness upon the face of the deep
God cracking the world in two with this
raw and angular music, 'round
midnight, and *it was good*

Pavane Pour Une Infante Défunte: Maurice Ravel

moment
before glass breaks, or then
again, before it
hardens in the making

liquid
state akin to longing, clarity
does not solidify to
pain, slow

and dark, her
breath, the notes go straight
to grief, a sorrow barely
tinted with delight, nervous

eyes, a bird
laid still in hand
half moon, the final
fall, before it

lifts
a passion
hatched inside the breast, and
fluttering

new spring blossoms, glazed
with ice, how
slow can slow

go, before it withers?
how deep can one note
drop, before it
dies?

In a Sentimental Mood: Duke Ellington

Melody is what takes your hand and leads you from this room into the next one.
                                                    Cheryl Jordan

Of course, moonlight
a smoky club and music sliding
out from the piano, from the sax, to color
the air. Your hand sliding
up my spine as we rocked together
barely moving—we called it dance
could it be that the same sentimental
tune went on and on, as I remember
combo rocking on the tiny stage for what
seemed hours, until you took my hand and led
me out the door into the city night so full
of possibility, each night stretching itself
into nights, the days between a faint golden
haze that links this mood to music, this
room to all the rooms stained with melody
with memory, vivid as hands sliding
down the strings, up my back, colliding
with the dark tangle of us

Everything seemed on the brink—the change of seasons, the coming of possibility.
Ethan Canin

Surprising tremolo from the strings or
my heart gone sentimental, remembering
those nights, when I took your hand
led you to the other room, the third body
we became as we rocked to our own
stained music, piano and sax, a smoky
bass, the mythical creature we were
several headed, serpent armed, double
voiced, response and counter, a melody
we would play for hours, no less
real now that what was once so sure, so
bodied is thin tangle of memory—your
hair rough on the pillow, my hands
caught in your hair, your hands sliding
soaked with smoke, with light, our sweat
and all the days between of possibility
a color, hazy with feeling and the dark
certainty of change

Instrumental II: James Taylor

a bell ringing
to no response, no
call to faith or arms
no child to grow

these simple chimes
a riff on solitude
that scrapes the meat
of grief away from bone

then bares her teeth
in laughter
before gobbling the
time she stole

Desafinado: Antonio Carlos Jobim

silk
dragged slow across the skin
        drying salted sand that edges sea
    or ruby light drawn deep from in the stone
          shaping
            space that sings *so cool and sways*
      her body feels
      the press of lips on sax
     stroke of fingers on the strings
  such smooth come hither tone
           that bends the newest green
              from notes and draws
  the sorry solid body from the sense of think
     to move into the sound
          feel it up
        from inside out

rhythm
full moon lifting tides between the legs
        as notes spill out the instruments to wet the air
  breathing sticks outside the beat
          but when
        this samba swings nothing stops
     the feet

Shine: Ford Dabney, Cecil Mack, Lew Brown

        I love
pomegranate flower
      for the hummingbird
lavender
      for the bees
static   for how it outlines movement
          and
you as perfect foil

    for me

Requiem, Op. 48: Gabriel Fauré

I. *Introit and Kyrie*

> *Requiem aeternam dona eis, Domine*
> Eternal rest grant them, O Lord
> > Latin mass for the dead

Life cascades toward death
        that clichéd drop
    down the falls in a barrel
  and if we survive the plunge
      O Lord
    who waits?
        crouching
   around the river's bend to
        take us down
when we're looking back, amazed
      when we're feeling our bones
  and blinking
    shivering and spewing
        pinching ourselves

who waits just as we ease out of that
        terrifying barrel
   exhausted
   into an ecstasy of disbelief

                              just when we're
            looking the other way
relieved
            and astonished
        and congratulating ourselves

            on a near miss

II. *Offertoire*

> *Ne cadant in obscurum*
> That they may not fall into darkness
>
> Latin mass for the dead

And the single form of this very thought
the single conjugation it makes in the future
tense, always edging around the perimeters of the room
feeling for the light switch that it
> *may not fall into darkness*

whisper thin and elusive, nudging the walls
of the self, elbowing its way from the back room your parents
once shared with their diseases and secrets, shouldering
its way to the front of the mind, each time in a new disguise
> (buying, sleeping, binging, lying)

rippling its way through the wet stream of self, plunging
in moments of respite
to shoot to the surface sleek headed again and again
gulping and dripping and into the house

III. *Sanctus*

> *Sanctus, Sanctus, Sanctus*
> Holy, Holy, Holy
>
> Latin mass for the dead

Yesterday, while watering, a small green hummingbird lighted
on the top rung of an empty tomato cage, inches from my face
he was still and inquisitive in the late light. His jet bead of a side
eye looked at me, or through me, and I was pinned, hose in hand

water arcing onto the sun-glazed santolina and sage

He was bobbing his head slightly in response to an easy breeze
but was otherwise quiet. As a child I was told that hummingbirds
could never rest, must always move lest their hearts explode
as death never rests, winging its way from flower to bright flower

unsatisfied, but he was at rest and I was at rest in him

Hose in hand and water falling, at rest for a moment, my ever
cranking soul suspended, my body, briefly body no more, but
something *holy*, reflected in that dark unblinking eye, until he
turned full face to look at me, then flew away

IV. *Pie Jesu*

> *Dona eis requiem*
> Grant them rest
>
> Latin mass for the dead

Have you noticed all the clothing we dress death in?

The stretch pants we pull on, flannel shirts, embarrassed
by its nude inevitability, we wrap a blanket around it
especially the unexpected, body dragged from the river
blank-faced girl found torn in a field, her skirt gone

And the explanations, the blame we place
she was depressed for a long time, he should have gotten
help, I told her not to go out at night, it was a fluke
as if anything could stop that speeding truck

We console ourselves with standard lines
the driver was thinking about his wedding, probably
on drugs, she refused to take her meds, he should have
she should have, they should have

Jesus, *grant them rest* from all the attempts to comprehend
to muffle that high-pitched sound rising on the edge of
consciousness, not gall, not grief, but naked truth, it could
have been me, it could have been me, it could have

V. *Agnus Dei*

> *Et lux perpetua luceat eis*
> And may perpetual light shine upon them
> Latin mass for the dead

A student once accused me of being morbid, being preoccupied with death but what else is worth such scrutiny, such concentration? Even love pales in fascination. After a few affairs one can almost anticipate the sequence of events the this and that of it. But death, no matter how we try to understand, it still eludes us, ferrets us out of hiding shines its perpetual light upon us

                                                Ha, found you!

Which reminds me of a story. A servant heard death would come for him that night. Terrified, he asked his master to tell all callers he was ill. Then he fled to Samarkand. When a stranger knocked and asked for the servant, the master said he was ill and could not be disturbed. Death laughed. No matter, I will see him at midnight in Samarkand. How this story nails us to our deepest fear

Our desire for assurance that we have time, that the knock is not for us . . .

                                                What! Now?

VI. *Libera Me*

> *Quando coeli movéndi sunt et terra*
> When the heavens and the earth shall quake
> Latin mass for the dead

What if, at 50, your mind suddenly starts to unravel, not unwind
like string from a spool, but unravel, each fiber untwisting
until the world you move through is fuzzy and without form
what if this happens slowly, so you can watch. At first you can't
find your keys, forget what day it is, aren't sure what a spoon is for
pretty soon you doubt your simplest thought, wonder if events
are happening or have happened or are yet to be. What if this
causes a kind of shaking in your soul, a sudden tremor in all you
thought was given, *the heavens and earth shall quake,* and startled by
your own life you want nothing more than to curl into sleep, hide
from your brain that slips between the telling of things. What if you
wake one morning having fallen off the bed of remembering in an
unfamiliar room, transformed not into a giant cockroach but into
the same self lesser, the same self without luster, the same *something
that is also something else, but what, and what*

VII. *In Paradisum*

> *Aeternam habeas requiem*
> Mayst thou have eternal rest
> Latin mass for the dead

Pirouette body does around this pivot called death
loops and long arcs of acceptance broken by fear

It's the best we can do, this lifting toward spirit, toward
blankness, toward transparency just to fall again

Each coil a return to genesis, time before the apple and fig
flaming streaks we sometimes see at sunset, claret rising

Against turquoise and azure, infinite arch the big bang
made when it split the universe into hemispheres

Those fragile moments when we *rest* in the belief that
eternity expands from us and outward to paradise

Kol Nidrei, Op. 47, Adagio on Hebrew Melodies: Max Bruch

> *All vows and oaths, all promises and obligations, all renunciations and responses that we shall make from this Day of Atonement until the next—may it come to us in peace—all of them we retract. May we be absolved of them all, may they all be null and void, may they be of no effect.*
>
> Kol Nidrei prayer

Day One

One long adagio
roan leaves dappling a still green pond
always autumn, with its sloping down to death
      when the year begins, or evening
beginning of our sacred day
tang of tears that fall into the hands
beneath the shawl in all the rocking prayer
to *daven* is to pray, to bend, to weave and moan
and look inside ourselves for supplication
but in it spirit soars, inside this fisted gesture
its hypnotic rubbed gold tone, a tallowy melody
is born. No whimper is lost, no umbered groan

Day Two

A silvered skein weaving generations now unstrung
on all but his one night when even those of us who
wander find our way back home, pale and tender
we return to what we've always been, beneath a cloth
that could be wing or shroud, in our simple cluster
flyspecks on the wall of time, the source of our
deep longing, distant and without name

Day Three

The recitative of orchestra and cello, a violin
high above the stony sound that draws pogrom
draws Palestine. All year we tune toward this one
night, into this symphony of soul, the minor
key that sounds our history transfigured now as
God with his transit and his pen surveys our deeds
waits until the final hour to write or cross us
from the book of life. We break our year worn
chrysalis, unfold these wet and crumpled wings, each
year again we're born back into *aleph*, with which
the world begins

Day Four

The world beings with *aleph*, the a afflicts
our souls, is amplified each year in apology and awe
we act as angels, dress in white, do not anoint
ourselves, abandon our accumulated sins, that animal
nature Moses broke upon the rock
in action, absolute and written, we are able, all
night, all day to stand at prayer without anger, affected
by how alive we feel again and what lies ahead, what
arises in this prayer where we ask nothing, are
assured even less. It is acceptance we lean into, our
Adonai afloat midair, an atmosphere where every arc
of every action is accounted for without accident and
when we make annulment of our vows, it is awe
runs through our arteries, as God appears we speak
His name out loud. We stand among our own
those we have wandered among always, and with an
absolute and perfect pitch we sing *amen*

Day Five

> I AM BECOMING WHO I AM BECOMING
> The name of God

Days of Awe
cirrus clouds, there is
high movement as the veil
thins and we near the night
we face our God and call
His name, which is not name

Day Six

The music of our long wandering
a silent prayer passed down the blood
across continents and seas, a God
who arranges us like notes, watches
our extermination and yet we bow
there is no explanation for a covenant
like ours. Abducted by the world
day after day for one whole year, as
autumn crests we turn our face, return
a capella, each by each, enter into
abstinence, sweetened with the honey
of repentance and regret. We
come into the temple abstracted
by loss and fear and God sings out our
names, each tone at will, and those who
hear become a wick of flame

Day Seven

We respond in prayer, a smoke
that curls into the ear of God
rides on a wailing melody
this tone that built the temple
digs the grave. The Greek gods
fed upon ambrosia, craved the scent
of burning meat, but our God
feeds on music, a chorus of us
bowed, but on our feet

Day Eight

Each rise precedes a fall
but as the elders say:
that's what knees are for

Day Nine

A light and slow opening moan
grandfathers in the temple chanting grace
their faces hidden, their everyday accents
gone in this river of Hebrew, the ancient tongue
hewn from music and pain. It is
duration. It is loss. It is forgetting and it is
wandering that makes us strong, we
become a prayer in time, an overtone
layment of word upon word, pure sounds
one atop the next like bodies in mass graves
or pebbles laid on ruined headstones
we return to what is fundamental year and again
when the moon turns from sliver to oval, and
atmosphere thins so we can look into the face of God
His name was lost long centuries ago, this left us
wandering each inside our own baleful prayer
forgiveness comes in the calling of His unknown
name, in such a delicate voice we do not profane

Day Ten

> *We are Your bespoken, and You are our Bespoken.*
> Kol Nidrei chant

All vows be broken like a cello string
split like a drying reed, leave the body
scraped of sound, exhausted by repentance
endless pathos and lament

All vows be broken this night when
One who plays us like an instrument
becomes our equal, our bespoken, radiant
before the dark to which the season bends

All vows, this holy night be broken
our breathing, a silent standing prayer
His fingering upon our strings alight with
possibility, as clean we rise into an infinite air

Aegean Sea: Vasilis Dimitriou

I was 21, I was
        in a rowboat
I was on a tour of the Aegean
              given by an unnamed Greek
I was shy
I did not speak my mother's tongue
        did not know what
I was doing in a boat with a man
I did not know
I was afraid of the water, among most things

I, who could not swim, suddenly
        and without warning, jumped, fully
    clothed into the Aegean
I was unprepared for this act
    as if it was not my own volition
        as if some
              ancestor had grabbed me by the shirt
            flung me
        from the boat shouting

      jump!
          this is life!
  this is all there is!

        suddenly flattened by
    an indescribable vastness
          that spread into every moment of the
I that no longer existed was the most
              satisfying place to be
      simple *it* inside sea and sky
my guide, who also no longer existed
                laughing and clapping in the boat
        both of us, unnamed now
           and the rolling, rowboat rocking
             and the breeze

Fantasia on a Theme by Thomas Tallis: Ralph Vaughan Williams

>   Thomas Tallis (c. 1505-1585)
>   Ralph Vaughan Williams (1872-1958)

Trees clutch night longest
tugged darkly onto limbs like sleeves
until maroon bark thins to red, then
hammered gold, to shine in early stars
of sun through woodland canopy

A dark incised by grace that cuts
the true from idyll green, leaf by leaf
serrates the trees, the clouds—lost notes
intoned above a melody handed man
to man across the centuries

Hymn and pastoral, a morning song
especially of birds that rise into the sky
like single notes of praise, sunder night
from day, from meditation on what has
been to benediction for what is yet to be

Sonata No. 14 in C-sharp Minor, Quasi una Fantasia, Op. 27, No. 2 (*Moonlight*): Ludwig van Beethoven

I. *Adagio sostenuto*

>*a feeling of* and, *a feeling of* if, *a feeling of* but, *and a feeling of* by
>William James

and *if by*   and *if by*   and *if by*
    chance, three notes sustain as time
    without edge, turn feeling

    as when two make one: *she* *and* *me*
        (*but* only *if* . . .)

        then leave one, solo instrument: *she* *and* *he*
                how the heart turns!
        from something singing to something played
abandons body, scatters
    feeling in its wake, like leaves in autumn moonlight, *by*
    a lake, they say, that one has never

        seen, dim sound at the shore of hearing
              (*but* only in memory . . .)

and if by   *and if by*   moving
    through me, turns air to body, body
        to liquid sound

                moonlight, they call it

    and all the days gone *by*

II. *Allegretto*

> *The sleep of reason produces monsters.*
> Goya

only in sleep does agony abate

    in sleep, partnered by piano
        whose keys are stairs

            that moonlight floats
      in memory
          or dream as heart

        floats, unmoored after ages
           tied to sound

    s t a i r s
one
    two   three

of graying cypress, cupped and twisting that we took
    flying, those nights, to the lake

        our hearts, bobbing

        like notes above the piano
    a small boat tied to the dock or
                        terns we watched as sun rose
  lined like stair
steps on the deep green
              fabric of the lake in sleep, it seemed

  in sleep where agony abates

III. *Presto agitato*

Some huge electrical phenomenon in which the immense quantity of energy released forces every particle into an exact relationship with every other particle.
Uncredited copywriter

they call it moonlight this
agitation, urgent notes exploding in
my brain, insistent ringing in the ears
maddening music to a frenzy
reticular as nerves that even now
begin to close to sound

how is it then, this instrument of mine
the strings are tuned toward silence
turning into almost sound, pounding
until they do not resonate, this fading
even worse than isolation in the world
of hearing still to come

insistent, fingers crashing at the keys
I ask my god why me? why steal
a gift once given, dull sounds that
note the borders of my being, why
make of me a conduit for what I will
not hear, a wire taut and vibrating

electric force that you set loose
charges into grace as melody, music

like no other, driving down, diminishing
sound, they call it moonlight, damn
them, damn their idylls, scattered leaves
damn eternal love and birds, asleep

damn this air thick with tones shattered
against a stone that once was ear, an
almost fantasy, like almost sound this liquid
lightning pouring through my hands
dimming, even as it hits the keys, they say
moonlight, idiots, how can they know

a constant storm grows inside my head
whirls daily toward its silent eye faster, faster
into bitter moonless night and still they call
it moonlight, *moonlight*, this force impossibly
contained in pale reflected light glinting off
that distant lake in which the music dies

Lullaby: George Gershwin

> *There is a whole order of insects, the mayflies, which we, whose life spans we've made the standard, have named the Ephemerata because we regard them as so short lived: adults last a day, two at the most. If stones did the naming, we'd be Ephemerata, too.*
>
> Sue Hubbell

Sleep, that crusts the corner of an eye
Sleep, that slides a film upon the teeth
Sleep, that gathers edges of a life
                      folds the blanket we call time

    sleep awhile my darling, sleep

Sleep, that pleats the curtain over day
Sleep, that irons creases on the face
Sleep, that rumples hair, unknots the mind
                      stops completely at red lights

    sleep awhile my darling, sleep

Sleep, that hides a basket in the rushes
Sleep, that rocks us even as we weep
Sleep, that bends the knife blade of desire
                      peppers caution onto fire

    sleep awhile my darling, sleep

Sleep, that waxy orchid of despair
Sleep, that drinks the absinthe of neglect
Sleep, that soaks the bitter out of fear
                              scars the lily, grinds the spice

       sleep awhile my darling, sleep

Sleep, that forms a quintet of the senses
Sleep, that bathes us in sea-colored light
Sleep, that slowly cobwebs conversation
                              winks us into infinite night

       sleep awhile my darling, sleep

Sleep, that buckles worry to regret
Sleep, that clings to leachy afternoon
Sleep, that lawny fabric of intent
                              gleaming spirit know as death

       sleep my darling, sleep awhile

Carly and Carole: Eumir Deodato

When I see equations, I see the letters in colors—I don't know why.
Richard Feynman

Lighthearted, a Brazilian beat, makes multicolored
    fabric, snapped against the sky
        argent music, coral and dun

            tinted iridescent by the sea's last light
    or glistening oyster in morning fog, opaline
the celadon of cello, aqua of guitar and drums
          a deeper green—loden or nile
    the bass, dark caramel tone, percussion
        ginger   nutmeg   clove

There's sand in this song, an alabaster beach
    blanched shells and bodies glazed with salt
        reflected in the trumpets tawny notes
            high above the periwinkle stain
        of French horn and trombone

No barbs or wrinkles, no warps or knobs
    cerulean sound, the sea at
            noontime, smooth and scissile, indigo
        edged with ivory and pearl, gossamer
fabric, flaring at the sky, flashing color

            ocean music, lucent and alive

Two Studies on Ancient Greek Scales: Harry Partch

And we too   we are made at least in part
*   of what we are not*
        Michael Ventura

What string is this that pulls me toward the sound of long horizon
      paralleling sea, an odd compelling harmony
        transects my heart, divides it from the present
and lifts me back into a mythic memory

Like cracks in coal or slits inside the rock or omphalos hid deep
      in ancient temple, this voice beneath my voice
        marks ground where my ancestors sang
this instrumental plainchant plaintive as their own

A body breathing in another room, another time, another inspiration
      exhalation, another body's cadence somehow
        mine, familiar as a sound still of the house
the wail viola makes, the thrumping cello strings

This five-tone humming flutters in the breast, like saddened cry
      of some imaginary beast, the whine of wooden
        instruments swelling near the sea, how far these
five tones travel, what terrain they gather

In their intonation, the whole of sky, antiquity to now and mountains
    as they undulate to sea, a final image rises
    to the mind: a line of dancers all in white
turning slowly, in an amphitheater, bending at the knee

Thanksgiving: George Winston

Love is so short, forgetting is so long.
Pablo Neruda

        crescent moon:
a brief inharmonious affair, nicks
the fabric of memory like this
crescent moon:
    shining pale autumnal light, insubstantial
        moon, hangs against the dotted swiss
stars make of sky, cold slice of
crescent moon:
   in the corner of night
     silver seam, a fading scar
         still tender, end of
autumn, branches clicking at the window
a thin and sickled tune, a
      crescent moon: almost gone
         to dark, a brief affair but sharp
like unexpected intake of autumnal air
a tear along the selvage of the heart, a cut like
      crescent moon: this
crescent moon

The Four Seasons: Antonio Vivaldi

Op. 8, Concerto No. 1 in E Major: *Primavera* [Spring]

> *E quindi sul fiorito ameno prato*
> And now in the pleasant flowery meadow
> Antonio Vivaldi

He wonders why we call it falling
when it's more like flying, like
seeds splitting their skins to become
something new, something bigger
like buds straining to open, like
spring in all her colored clothes

First snowdrops of the season
winter edging out the door, then
crocus, then hyacinth, then jonquil
and narcissus before the daffodils
before the tulips, before the violets
finally, polka dot the grass

A milky sky, the sharpest green
almost yellow buds on trees still bare
of flower, leaf and fruit, all is possibility
before the weight of knowing, before
the weight of summer bends branches
toward the ready earth

Op. 8, Concerto No. 2 in G Minor: *L'Estate* [Summer]

> *Toglie alle membra lasse il suo riposo*
> His weary limbs are deprived of rest
> Antonio Vivaldi

He calls to say he's fallen, but
she's unsure, she asks for time
some months, but he is frantic, his
heart gallops, his brain, what did he
do to turn her away, what should
he do, what can he do but wait?

Summer drags, lush and heavy, a deepening
green and moving air through leaves that
catch the light in layered geometric, languid
days and fretful nights deprived of rest
from parched to drenched, the sky, his
mind, full of insects, humming

His heart flutters at the top of his breast, as
leaves flutter on doomed plane trees all across
France, he thinks of those trees and birds, that
flutter as they settle on the nest. The plums ripen
he remembers a summer truth, withhold water
sweeter fruit, withhold love—longing

Op. 8, Concerto No. 3 in F Major: *L'Autunno* [Autumn]

> *E' la staggion ch'invita tanti e tanti*
> It is the season that invites one and all
>   Antonio Vivaldi

Summer's sunk her teeth into the trees
will not budge. The heat holds on, leaves
hold on, not even burnished at the tips and
still she does not call. His heart swells like fruit
presses the breath from his chest, late plums
ripen, darken, sweeten, soften, then fall

Very slow the season goes, the pages
turn, the leaves take up their work, go gold
then litter the earth. The gate is closed, but
not before the final mums and marigolds
are gathered with the single pumpkin
thick skinned and bright as resolve

So much work this season, who can
heed the grieving heart? There's wood
to split, a roof to fix and every hole to seal
sometimes he almost stops mid-swing, ax
in arc against the sky, he sees her face
he lets the blade fell it from his mind

Op. 8, Concerto No. 4 in F Minor: *L'Inverno* [Winter]

> *Per timor di cader, girsene intenti*
> For fear of falling, turning cautiously
>   Antonio Vivaldi

He prays for snow, or anything that falls
makes a blanket for this pain, leaves no trace, no
scar save certain rivulets, when melting into earth
wind blows hard against the house, branches scratch
like animals that ask to be let in, let out, let in, he
feels the winter turning inside, out, then in

It's quiet here inside the house, inside
the sound of rain that falls against the walls
against the roof, against the needles of the pine
rain that runs into the gutters clogged with autumn
leaves and rotted plums, rain that overflows
melts the pain that hardened into ice

He feels the early stirring, like a beak inside
an egg tap tapping, something living moves
inside his chest. He feels the solid plum seed
crack to root, feels the ready earth inside, feels
a wing lifting against the sky, he calls it falling
calls it falling, calls it flying into life

Synchrony No. 2: Moondog (Louis Hardin)

Blue snow light
sharpens every branch

hieroglyphs the trees
against the night

sugared face of
crayon colored iris

head barely raised
above the white

Notes on the Music

Writing this book was a rare and gorgeous experience. Following the notes within the movements, the movements within the music, and the poems from piece to piece was revelatory, exciting, frustrating and, at times, awe-invoking. Each poem traveled *to* me, *through* me, and onto the page. I hope this engagement is evident, and that the poems compel the reader to return to the music—to listen again, or for the first time.

The following notes identify and comment on the renditions I listened to when writing the poems.

Aegean Sea: Vasilis Dimitriou. I know little about this strangely resonant piece, which I listen to on a 1980 General Publishing Company tape, with the liner notes in Greek.

Capriccio in C-sharp Minor, Op. 76: Johannes Brahms. I first heard this piece played by my dear friend and wonderful musician Anca Manu, in her living room in Rotterdam, Holland. I begged her to let me record her playing, which she did. Her rendition is still the definitive for me. In an effort to extend the life of that cherished tape, I also listen to a recording by Julius Katchen on the London CD *Johannes Brahms Works for Solo Piano*, recorded sometime between 1962 and 1965.

Carly and Carole: Eumir Deodato. I spent several years in the 1980s teaching aerobics at the Hollywood YMCA. This piece, from Deodato's album *Prelude*, was a favorite of the fitness crowd. The album has a notable line-up of jazz musicians including Eumir Deodato on piano, Ron Carter on bass, Stanley Clarke on electric bass, Airto on percussion, and Hubert Laws on flute.

Desafinado: Antonio Carlos Jobim. I love Brazilian jazz, especially when played by Stan Getz. The 1963 Verve recording of Getz, João Gilberto, and Antonio Carlos Jobim tops my list. I also listen to the recording on the Ken Burns *Jazz* CD of Stan Getz with Charlie Byrd from the 1962 album *Jazz Samba*.

Fantasia on a Theme by Thomas Tallis: Ralph Vaughan Williams. I listen to two versions: A 1976 EMI Classics recording of the London Philharmonic with Sir Adrian Boult; and a CBS Great Performances CD titled *Romantic Favorites for Strings*, Leonard Bernstein conducting the New York Philharmonic. The Bernstein was recorded in either 1964 or 1971 (the CD is poorly labeled). I chose the CD initially for the first piece, Samuel Barber's Adagio for Strings, which I intended to write about. But every time I played the CD, the Fantasia prevailed.

The Four Seasons: Antonio Vivaldi. The LP I wore out in college had a white cover with brightly colored text. That's all I remember. Now I listen to Seiji Ozawa with the Boston Symphony Orchestra, Joseph Silverstein on violin, Telarc, 1982; The London Symphony Orchestra, Alexander Barantschik on violin, Fine Classics, 1999; and Nadja Salerno-Sonnenberg with the Orchestra of St. Lukes, EMI, 1990.

In a Sentimental Mood: Duke Ellington. Michael Ventura made me the most glorious set of tapes he titled *Ellington Heaven*, which follow Ellington's career across the decades. He included several versions of this song in the set. But my favorite, the one I listen to more than any other, is the 1962 recording of Ellington and John Coltrane on the Ken Burns *Jazz* CD. I can't get over how Ellington has Coltrane carry the piece, his piano a quiet river running behind that saxophone. Sheer genius.

Instrumental II: James Taylor. A lyrical little piece found on Taylor's *One Man Dog* album. I listened to it again and again and again as an adolescent. That music saved me.

Kol Nidrei, Op. 47, Adagio on Hebrew Melodies: Max Bruch. Haunting. The version I listen to most is the 1936 recording of Pablo Casals with the London Symphony Orchestra under Sir Landon Ronald on Pearl Records—a heartfelt, majestic, and plaintive rendition.

Köln Concert: Keith Jarrett. There is only one concert, recorded live. The first seven notes are an astonishing experience. Every time.

Lullaby: George Gershwin. What an alluring composition. I listen to it on the 1994 Sony CD *Gershwin Greatest Hits*. No recording date is listed for the piece, which is played by the Juilliard String Quartet.

Pavane Pour Une Infante Défunte: Maurice Ravel. This is my favorite music-finding story. I was working with a group of architecture apprentices, at the Frank Lloyd Wright School of Architecture, on a humanities project. Their goal was to translate and perform a set of 19th century French poems about childhood. The group decided—at the eleventh hour—to include music of the same century. Live, solo piano music. Knowing little to nothing about French music history, we went to the local Borders bookstore to check out the sheet music, and chose this piece because it had "infante" in the title and fit the geographical and period constraints. The poor pianist (another architecture apprentice who had agreed to play) had only a week to learn what was, I found out, a very difficult piece. But he pulled it off, and the evening was enchanting. Since then I listen to the VoxBox *Ravel: Complete Music for Solo Piano*, with Abby Simon, pianist.

Requiem, Op. 48: Gabriel Fauré. I love requiems. The Fauré, often described as the "happy" requiem, is my favorite. There are two versions I listen to interchangeably: A 1975 EMI recording of the Edinburgh Festival Orchestra directed by Daniel Barenboim, and a 1983 Harmonia Mundi recording of the work played by La Chapelle Royale/Ensemble Musique Oblique, directed by Philippe Herreweghe.

'Round Midnight: Thelonious Monk. I listen to many versions—by Monk himself and other great musicians. I love the Blue Note recording of Monk playing, but the version I currently find most compelling is by the Kronos Quartet with Ron Carter, on the Landmark CD *Kronos Quartet Monk Suite*.

Shine: Ford Dabney, Cecil Mack, Lew Brown. Never heard of these composers? Nor had I. So I scoured jazz history until I found a brief mention in Gary Giddins' book *Visions of Jazz*. On page 45 Giddins writes, "Most listeners will likely recognize the names of the white composers now embedded in a Golden Age pantheon that generally admits of only three African Americans (W.C. Handy, Duke Ellington and Fats Waller). Yet other songs of universal distinction are so completely sundered from their authors that people are invariably surprised to learn that they were written by black composers and lyricists. Consider the renown of the following and the obscurity of their makers: . . . "Shine" (Ford Dabney and Cecil Mack); . . . ."

Shine is part of the soundtrack to Woody Allen's film *Sweet and Lowdown*, and Ry Cooder does a great version, but the one I think of first is a 1936 recording of *Django Reinhardt and Le Quartet du Hot Club de France* with Stéphane Grappelli on violin. Again, Ken Burns had the unerring taste to include this rendition on his *Jazz* CD.

Six Suites for Unaccompanied Cello: Johann Sebastian Bach.
The 1983 Yo Yo Ma recording on CBS is the one I always return to, although I also listen to a 1938 recording by Pablo Casals remastered by EMI in 1988.

Sonata No. 14 in C-sharp Minor, *Quasi una Fantasia***, Op. 27, No. 2 (***Moonlight***): Ludwig van Beethoven.** The LP of my memory is long gone. It had a deep blue cover and featured Arthur Rubinstein on piano. It must have been recorded before or during the 1970s, because that was the decade I listened to it until the grooves were gone. Now, I listen to Rudolf Serkin's 1963 recording on a CBS *Great Performances* CD. I learned that Beethoven never called it "moonlight" and hated the title.

String Quartet in F Major, Op. 96 (*American***): Antonín Dvořák.** I first heard this piece played by the Talich Quartet at the Pablo Casals Music Festival in Prades, France in the summer of 2000. To say it brought tears to my eyes is an understatement. I now listen to a 1997 Harmonia Mundi recording by the Melos Quartet, but I long for a recording of that performance by the Talich.

String Quintet in C, Op. 163: Franz Schubert. I listen to a 1983 EMI recording of the Alban Berg Quartet with Heinrich Schiff on cello, but the piece first revealed itself to me in Prades. It was played in the 10th century Abbaye Saint Michel de Cuxa by a terrific quintet of Europeans from several countries. I was privileged to sit in on rehearsal, as well as attend the concert.

Synchrony No. 2: Moondog (Louis Hardin). Moondog is one of a kind—a composer who invented his own instruments, a street musician with a sweetly disorganized and dissonant sound. One either loves him or walks away. I find him oddly appealing. Although I have a recording of Moondog playing his own compositions, the piece I like best is from the Kronos Quartet's *Early Music* CD with Judith Sherman on drums.

Thanksgiving: George Winston. In general, so-called New Age music is not my style, but this CD is simply breathtaking. *December*, George Winston, Windham Hill, 1982.

Two Studies on Ancient Greek Scales: Harry Partch. Harry Partch designed and built his own instruments, primarily of wood, then composed pieces to play on them. This piece is an arrangement by Ben Johnston played by the Kronos Quartet on their *Early Music* CD, recorded between 1993 and 1997. The particular form of the piece as Partch wrote it (five tones played on a four-string instrument) advised the poem's form.

Acknowledgements

Habent sua fata libelli [books have their own fates]—not just after their publication, but especially during their creation.
                                                                Thomas Mann

This Music is on the cusp of adolescence—it's been almost thirteen years since the idea for the book came to me in a quiet house in the fir and madrone woodland of Northern California. During those years, some poems made their way into journals, other poems were cut from the manuscript, sequencing was considered, changed, and changed back. Musician extraordinaire Cory Wright collaborated with me on a performance that brought the poems to life in voice and sound. So many years ... so much gratitude.

Many people listened to or read the manuscript. Thank you Michael Fruta, Paula Gocker, Cheryl Jordan, Ted Peterson, Michael Ventura, and the Willits Book Group—Fran Resendez, Carlin Diamond, Tui McCarthy, Nancy Horrocks, Marilyn Darrow, Donna Kerr, Marcia Pratt—for encouraging and clarifying the work.

The following people introduced me to the music; without them, this book would not exist. Thank you Yiannis Adamopoulos for the Köln Concert, Ari Georges for the Bach Cello Suites, Cheryl Jordan for the fantastic Ry Cooder version of Shine (as well as for explanations of musical composition), Anca Manu for the Brahms Capriccio, the late John Wyatt for the Fauré Requiem. I am eternally grateful to Anca Manu and Frans Pauw for inviting me to the Prades Music Festival and to Vlady and Marika Mendelssohn for making the experience possible.

Thank you Eric Farnsworth for 19th century farming facts, Andreas Symietz for sending me copies of classical sheet music from Germany, and Franz Enciso at the UC Berkeley Music Library for all your assistance. I am also indebted to Ken Burns for his wonderful *Jazz* series, and to Mike A'Dair who turned me on to Geoff Dyer's book *But Beautiful*, which inspired this work.

John Amarantides. Your enthusiastic and unwavering belief in me was essential to this work. You are the artist I aspire to become. My thanks to you are evergreen.

Michael, Jazmin, and all the fine folks at LettersAt3amPress. How can I express my appreciation? Working with you was extraordinary. You are changing the way publishing works and I am honored to be part of the adventure.

Friends, family, colleagues, students—every one of you has advanced this work by enriching my life.

And, of course, enduring gratitude to the work itself, which sustains me.

The following poems have quotes incorporated into the text:

'Round Midnight: Thelonious Monk
"Darkness upon the face of the deep" and "it was good" are from the *King James Bible*, Genesis, Chapter 1.

Desafinado: Antonio Carlos Jobim
"So cool and sways" is from "The Girl from Ipanema," Portuguese lyrics by Vinicius de Moraes, English lyrics by Norman Gimbel.

Requiem, Op. 48: Gabriel Fauré
"Something that is also something else, but what, and what" is from *The Body Artist* by Don DeLillo. Scribner, 2001. p. 36.

About the Author

Karen Holden is a poet, artist, and educator.

Published widely, her work crosses disciplines. *Book of Changes* is a volume of 64 poems based on the ancient Chinese text *I Ching*, and the limited edition *How Love Comes Home: Los Angeles in Four Voices* weaves family story into the history of Los Angeles through poetry, essays, and images. "Quartet for Desert Moon"—a poem commissioned by the Los Angeles County Museum of Art—is included in the museum's permanent collection mobile tour. She recently completed another series of poems for the museum.

A native Los Angelina, Karen works in higher education communications, and teaches persuasive and creative writing at museums, schools, and professional conferences.

www.ingramcontent.com/pod-product-compliance
Lightning Source LLC
Chambersburg PA
CBHW032046290426
44110CB00012B/981